LIFE AS AN AIRCRAFT TECHNICIAN

LIFE AS AN AIRCRAFT TECHNICIAN

A Brief Look Through The Eyes of 42 Years of Experience in The Demanding Aviation Maintenance Profession.

R.C. WITBECK (ACETECH)

WILL FIX
AIRPLANES
FOR
BEER

Disclaimer

In this industry and profession, practices are constantly changing. This book only offers a basic understanding of this career. Do not rely on statements made in this book due to the fact that they are of a fictional nature. What is written in this book is a single and personal perspective from an individual with 42 years of aircraft maintenance experience and training.

ACKNOWLEDGMENTS

First and foremost, I would like to thank God for keeping me in sound mind to write this book. Secondly, my caring and loving parents who gave me encouragement and a foundation to enter this wonderful career. May their souls rest in peace. Lastly, all of my technical instructors who believed in me and helped me obtain my Federal Aviation Administration Airmen's License and degree, all of my family, friends, mentors, co-workers, leads, supervisors, managers, directors, and union brothers who played an intricate part in who I am today.

1

WHEN THE DREAM STARTED

As a very young boy, I noticed the joy in working with my hands. Even before that, I would watch my dad do the maintenance on his 1948 33-foot Chris Craft Sedan yacht because he couldn't afford to pay to have it done. I used to collect old bicycles that the neighbors threw away. Exchange parts to make a good-running bike. Once I started driving, the water pump went out on my dad's 1971 Ford Galaxy 500. Since mom and I shared this vehicle, I had to cover the maintenance and fuel. The water pump change was a success and, yes, by my way! However, I felt like I wanted something more than car repair. One day, while working on that old rusty Ford, a neighbor named Mr. McCoy (a painter by trade) encouraged me to consider aircraft maintenance based on his military experience. He said, "Go west to California. That's where all the aviation jobs are." And I listened to him. Mr. McCoy was my first career mentor. In my hometown, we had a school called Aviation High School. The program was designed for you to attend your last 3 years of high school during the second half of your school day. Once you graduate, you are eligible to take the FAA test. I never attended that school, but I still wanted that career, and that confirmed to my parents that I was serious. Two very expensive aviation schools came to our home and pitched their presentation. We agreed to a 2-year technical college within the state in order to take advantage of better cost saving opportunities along with financial aid. Coincidentally, around this time, there was a prediction of a large shortage of aviation techs due to the retirement of WW2 vets.

2

TECHNICAL COLLEGE... PARTYTIME! (1977)

My school was a 2-year technical college in Columbus, Ohio. Its aviation program was small but highly accredited. My first few months were tough. I didn't know a thing while sitting next to ex-military aircraft mechanics or other students who had been around aircraft before. I slowly got acclimated and didn't give up. I continued to work odd part-time jobs. One of my classmates sold his dad's car for $300.00. It was a faded green 1969 Buick Rivera, one-owner, in good shape. Hallelujah! What a blessing! At that same time, I had a part-time job working in a gas station. I was able to maintain it quite well with the auto repair shop I was employed in. I like a young man, it was great to be away from home on your own, especially moving to another city. School life was great. I got to meet a lot of interesting people, most of them being older. I found an apartment and a part-time job within walking distance of campus. Fortunately, I was not wild enough to let the pretty girls and drugs get in the way of thinking, just to a certain extent. I actually finished my technical training and obtained my FAA Airframe & Powerplant license. With a few non-technical classes to obtain the AA Degree, I went ahead and completed them to boot!

Case In Point

As a full-time technical college student, I didn't have much money. One Saturday night, my girlfriend and I were sitting around and board. I came up with the idea to go to my tech school, where the airplanes were sitting outside. We were able to climb into a Twin-engine Beech-18, an F-86 military jet, and a small Mooney aircraft. She was thoroughly delighted and had a really inexpensive date.

Columbus Technical Institute

hereby confers upon

Robert Crawford Witbeck

the degree of

Associate of Applied Science

together with all the rights, privileges, and honors appertaining thereto in consideration of the satisfactory completion of the Course prescribed in

Aviation Maintenance Technology

In Testimony Whereof, the seal of the Institute and the signatures as authorized by the Board of Trustees are hereunto affixed.

Given at Columbus, Ohio, this twelfth day of June 1981

David O Cox
Chairman of the Board of Trustees

Harold M. Menton
President

Timothy R. Strumph
Vice-Chairman of the Board of Trustees

David D. White
Secretary of the Board of Trustees

Columbus Technical Institute

hereby confers upon

Robert Crawford Witbeck

the certificate of

Air Frame

under the terms of Air Agency Certificate Number 4628

together with all the rights, privileges, and honors appertaining thereto in consideration of the satisfactory completion of the Course prescribed in

Aviation Maintenance Technology

In Testimony Whereof, the seal of the Institute and the signatures as authorized by the Board of Trustees are hereunto affixed.

Given at Columbus, Ohio, this *eighth* day of *June 1979*

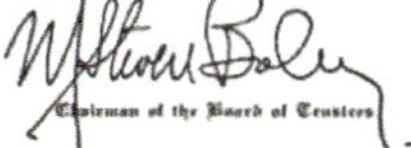

Chairman of the Board of Trustees

President

Secretary of the Board of Trustees

Columbus Technical Institute

hereby confers upon

ROBERT CRAWFORD WITBECK

the certificate of

Powerplant

under the terms of Air Agency Certificate Number 4628

together with all the rights, privileges, and honors appertaining thereto in consideration of the satisfactory completion of the Course prescribed in

Aviation Maintenance Technology

In Testimony Whereof, the seal of the Institute and the signatures as authorized by the Board of Trustees are hereunto affixed.

Given at Columbus, Ohio, this *14th* day of *December 1979*

Chairman of the Board of Trustees

President

Secretary of the Board of Trustees

AIRMAN WRITTEN TEST REPORT (RIS: AC 8080-2)

DO NOT DESTROY THIS TEST REPORT — This Test Report must be presented for retesting or certification.

DEPARTMENT OF TRANSPORTATION · FEDERAL AVIATION ADMINISTRATION

SSN   3316   16

TEST		GRADES BY SECTION							FAA OFFICE NO.	TEST DATE	EXPIRATION DATE	
TAKE NO.	TITLE *	1	2	3	4	5	6	7				
01	AMG	92							GL 07	06-22-79		
EXPIRATION DATE (last day of month)		681										

* See codes on reverse side.

MECHANICS ONLY - EXPIRATION DATE CODES

The first character designates the month; the second and third characters, the year. January through September as shown by numbers 1 through 9; October as "O"; November as "N"; December as "D".

LAST NAME, FIRST MIDDLE

EXAMPLES:
Month (June) — 6
Year (1975) — 75
Month (December) — D
Year (1975) — 75

NOTE: TO FIND THE SUBJECT AREA IN WHICH QUESTIONS WERE MISSED, COMPARE THE CODES SHOWN BELOW WITH THE CODED ITEMS ON THE ENCLOSED SUBJECT AREA OUTLINE.

SECTION	SUBJECT AREA CODES
1	A04 B02 C02 E01

FRAUDULENT ALTERATION OF THIS FORM BY ANY PERSON IS A BASIS FOR SUSPENSION OR REVOCATION OF ANY CERTIFICATES OR RATINGS HELD BY THAT PERSON.

AC FORM 8080-2 (6-76)

ISSUED BY: ADMINISTRATOR FEDERAL AVIATION ADMINISTRATION

AIRMAN WRITTEN TEST REPORT (RIS: AC 8080-2)

DO NOT DESTROY THIS TEST REPORT — This Test Report must be presented for retesting or certification.

DEPARTMENT OF TRANSPORTATION · FEDERAL AVIATION ADMINISTRATION

SSN   3321   14

TEST		GRADES BY SECTION							FAA OFFICE NO.	TEST DATE	EXPIRATION DATE	
TAKE NO.	TITLE *	1	2	3	4	5	6	7				
01	AMA	80	71						GL 07	06-22-79		
EXPIRATION DATE (last day of month)		681	681									

* See codes on reverse side.

MECHANICS ONLY - EXPIRATION DATE CODES

The first character designates the month; the second and third characters, the year. January through September as shown by numbers 1 through 9; October as "O"; November as "N"; December as "D".

LAST NAME, FIRST MIDDLE

EXAMPLES:
Month (June) — 6
Year (1975) — 75
Month (December) — D
Year (1975) — 75

NOTE: TO FIND THE SUBJECT AREA IN WHICH QUESTIONS WERE MISSED, COMPARE THE CODES SHOWN BELOW WITH THE CODED ITEMS ON THE ENCLOSED SUBJECT AREA OUTLINE.

SECTION	SUBJECT AREA CODES
1	D02 D04 D05 D06 F02
2	K01 L03 M02 M03 N02 O01 O03 P01 P06 Q01 Q02 Q03 R02 T01

FRAUDULENT ALTERATION OF THIS FORM BY ANY PERSON IS A BASIS FOR SUSPENSION OR REVOCATION OF ANY CERTIFICATES OR RATINGS HELD BY THAT PERSON.

AC FORM 8080-2 (6-76)

ISSUED BY: ADMINISTRATOR FEDERAL AVIATION ADMINISTRATION

DO NOT DESTROY THIS TEST REPORT. This Test Report must be presented for retesting or certification.	DEPARTMENT OF TRANSPORTATION • FEDERAL AVIATION ADMINISTRATION — AIRMAN WRITTEN TEST REPORT (RIS: AC 8080-2)	4780	15
		SSN	

TEST		GRADES BY SECTION							FAA OFFICE NO.	TEST DATE	EXPIRATION DATE
TAKE NO.	TITLE *	1	2	3	4	5	6	7			
01	AMP	84	79						GL 06	01-02-80	
EXPIRATION DATE (Last day of month)		182	182								

* See codes on reverse side:

◄———————————— MECHANICS ONLY - EXPIRATION DATE CODES

The first character designates the month; the second and third characters, the year. January through September as shown by numbers 1 through 9; October as "O"; November as "N"; December as "D".

LAST NAME, FIRST MIDDLE

EXAMPLES:
Month (June) ____ 6
Year (1975) ____ 75
Month (December) ____ D
Year (1975) ____ 75

NOTE: TO FIND THE SUBJECT AREA IN WHICH QUESTIONS WERE MISSED, COMPARE THE CODES SHOWN BELOW WITH THE CODED ITEMS ON THE ENCLOSED SUBJECT AREA OUTLINE.

SECTION	SUBJECT AREA CODES
1	A01 A02 C01
2	H01 H02 I01 K03 L01 M02 N01 P02 Q02 R05

UNAUTHORIZED REPRODUCTION OF THIS FORM BY ANY PERSON MAY RESULT IN SUSPENSION OR REVOCATION OF ANY CERTIFICATES OR RATINGS HELD BY SUCH PERSON.

AC FORM 8080-2 (6-76)

ISSUED BY: ADMINISTRATOR, FEDERAL AVIATION ADMINISTRATION

I. UNITED STATES OF AMERICA — DEPARTMENT OF TRANSPORTATION—FEDERAL AVIATION ADMINISTRATION	III. CERTIFICATE NO.

II. TEMPORARY AIRMAN CERTIFICATE

THIS CERTIFIES THAT IV.

V.

DATE OF BIRTH	HEIGHT	WEIGHT	HAIR	EYES	SEX	NATIONALITY	VI.
09-24-58	72 IN.	150	BROWN	BROWN	M	USA	

IX. has been found to be properly qualified and is hereby authorized in accordance with the conditions of issuance on the reverse of this certificate to exercise the privileges of

MECHANIC

RATINGS AND LIMITATIONS

XII. AIRFRAME

XIII. POWERPLANT

THIS IS ☐ AN ORIGINAL ISSUANCE ☒ A REISSUANCE OF THIS GRADE OF CERTIFICATE

DATE OF SUPERSEDED AIRMAN CERTIFICATE
07-19-79

BY DIRECTION OF THE ADMINISTRATOR

EXAMINER'S DESIGNATION NO. OR INSPECTOR'S REG. NO.
1773239

DATE DESIGNATION EXPIRES
10-31-80

VII. AIRMAN'S SIGNATURE	X. DATE OF ISSUANCE	X. SIGNATURE OF EXAMINER OR INSPECTOR
	01-24-80	

FAA Form 8060-4 (4-69) Supersedes Previous Edition

U.S. Department
of Transportation

**Federal Aviation
Administration**

Certificate of Training
"Gold Award"
presented to

ROBERT WITBECK

*Has Satisfactorily Completed the Training Requirements for
the Gold Award*

Representative of the Administrator

December 31, 2005

Date

3

MY 1ˢᵀ JOBS IN AVIATION

One of my mentors suggested that I find a job related to my career. Amazingly, I did. It was an established FBO at the local airport. They serviced and repaired Cessna, Piper, and Beechcraft planes. I was hired as the *"hangar clean-up"* guy. This was an awesome opportunity! Once I got all my clean-up stuff done, I would offer to help the experienced technicians and gain invaluable knowledge. While working there, a company merger took place from another FBO across the airport. My boss must have been fond of me. He said, *"Son, you are now a technician with this new merger, go buy yourself some tools."* I asked him about my school. He said, *"Just come to work after you're done with your classes."* At that time, I had no license.

A good friend and classmate informed me that a Learjet charter and service center was hiring techs. No license was required if you were enrolled in an A & P school. I got hired! It was my 1st introduction to a union shop and shift work. I was able to finish school with that job. Did you know that the first Learjet engine (GE CJ-610) was the exact same engine as the military version (GE J-85) without the after burner? My third job was in Louisville, KY. It was a national FBO. I never experienced a major airport with a tractor factory on one side and a boat factory on the other!

I was hired solely based on my Learjet experience. At that time, I didn't realize how valuable that was. Their hangar consisted of several 20 & 30 series Learjets from different corporations. He said he will need me to assume the position of Lead Technician on these aircraft. I accepted the job. Being the home of the Kentucky Derby, airplanes and VIPs flew in from all over the world for this event every year. We had to close runways in order to handle the parking. I once spoke to a corporate pilot who flew for a company that makes millions of dollars "studding out" prize winning race horses. My 4th job was in Indianapolis, IN. This was a rather unique aviation operation. They advertised themselves as a *"Vacation Airline."* Their equipment consisted of large planes that flew to major cities all over the world, such as Madrid, Paris, Tokyo, etc. Non-stop round trip with hotel and tour guides included! Membership needed a fee that not many people could afford. However, this outfit was great for me. Now I can put the long-awaited aircraft on my resume, such as Boeing 707, 727, Lockheed L-1011, and McDonnell Douglas DC-10.

Case in Point

While working with the jet charter service in Columbus, OH, my brother came by bus to visit me. On his way back home, I was able to get him a free *"deadhead"* flight back to Cleveland, Ohio, on a 20 Series Learjet. When my dad came to pick him up, he was in tears.

One day, a technical college classmate hired on at my executive jet charter service. However, we couldn't understand why he came to work with my company. He had previously been hired right out of school by a corporate firm that maintained a few jets for the local gas company. I asked him, *"Why would you quit a great job like that?"* Well, he told me he didn't drink alcohol, but the whole maintenance staff did. I guess the grass isn't always greener.

On a Friday evening at the FBO, I was assigned to wash a Twin-engine Piper aircraft. While trying to hurry, I snapped an antenna off the belly of the plane with a cleaning brush. Oh God! What should I do? Like a little boy who made a boo-boo, I went and told the maintenance manager what happened. He said, *"No problem, we'll take care of it. It's good you came and told us now; if not, I would've fired you."*

Learjet 23

Learjet 24

SDF Airport "Kentucky Derby Weekend" 1982

4

FINALLY! A MAJOR AIRLINE JOB

I had an instructor in tech school tell me to get with a major airline if I want to make good money. I never forgot what was said. I am now 26. I used one of my current job's airplanes to fly to Palm Springs, CA, rented a car to Los Angeles, and applied at Continental Airlines. Upon returning to my current job, I got the call to return to LA on an employee applicant flight pass. My interview went pretty well due to the fact that I already had five years' experience, along with the exact aircraft they maintain. At that time, there were airline strikes.

Continental's strike was pretty much done. I got the job without having to cross a picket line. I started my first major airline job without a union. My job probation lasted 180 days. You can't be late for work, call in sick, or get caught sleeping on the job, or you will be fired. Obviously, I passed my probation.

Case in Point

While on probation, I was assigned to remove and replace a Boeing 727 windshield, which required two techs. It's over 2 inches thick and has over 30 bolts. The senior tech was on the outside, and I was on the inside. Suddenly, in the process, the windshield got chipped on the outside. I yelled at him, *"What are we going to do?"* He said, *"Don't worry about it."* The next day, the shift supervisor and crew planner rushed up to me and asked me one question: *"Did you work on the inside or outside?"* I told them inside, and that was the end of it. I didn't get fired.

Airbus A300

5

AIRCRAFT SPECIALTY SCHOOLS

There are many types of aircraft that airlines operate, depending on where they fly. Whether it be a jet charter company/FBO or a major operator that flies globally, every aircraft has its own specialty school. Some companies will send you to the factory or have an in-house training department with a staff of instructors. Some factory schools can last up to 6 months. Jet engine schools are needed in the overhaul facilities from companies such as General Electric or Rolls-Royce. In-house training schools range from one week (FAA minimum) to 8 weeks. Also called familiarization schools (fam-schools), they are a really great tool to start a new job. However, I think it's better to work on that particular aircraft first before going to school on it.

CERTIFICATE OF TRAINING

Awarded to

Robert C. Witbeck

who has satisfactorily completed the

US Air

BAC 1-11 Maintenance Initial

Training Program

Walter F. Bixler, Jr.
Contract Training

January 1984

Continental

Certificate of Training

Be it known that

Robert C. Witbeck

has successfully completed

MD-80 Avionics/Electrical (80 Hours)

on this ___6th___ day of ___March___ nineteen hundred and ___Ninety Eight___

Bob Torres
Instructor
Maintenance Training

Frank Steiner
Manager
Maintenance Training

McDonnell Douglass MD-80 Avionics/Electrical

Continental

Certificate of Training

Be it known that

ROBERT C. WITBECK

has successfully completed

B757-200/300 DIFFERENCES

on this **5TH** day of **MARCH**

2002

Instructor
Maintenance Training

Manager
Maintenance Training

Boeing 757–200/300 Differnces

CONTINENTAL AIRLINES

Certificate of Training

Be it known that

ROBERT C. WITBECK

has successfully completed

B727 A&P

on this ___29th___ day of ___August___ nineteen

hundred and ___Eighty-six___

Instructor
Maintenance Training

Manager
Maintenance Training

Boeing 727 Airframe and Powerplant

CONTINENTAL AIRLINES

Certificate of Training

Be it known that

BOB WITBECK

has successfully completed

A300 AVIONICS/ELECTRICAL

on this 23RD *day of* SEPTEMBER *nineteen*

hundred and EIGHTY-EIGHT

Instructor
Maintenance Training

Manager
Maintenance Training

Airbus A300 Avionics/Electrical

CONTINENTAL AIRLINES

Certificate of Training

Be it known that

ROBERT WITBECK

has successfully completed

DC-10 A&P

on this 15th *day of* November *nineteen*

hundred and Eighty-five

Instructor
Maintenance Training

Manager
Maintenance Training

McDonnell Douglas DC-10 Airframe and Powerplant

CONTINENTAL AIRLINES

Certificate of Training

Be it known that

ROBERT CRAWFORD WITBECK

has successfully completed

DC-10 Avionics

on this 26th *day of* September *nineteen*

hundred and Eighty-six

Instructor
Maintenance Training

Manager
Maintenance Training

McDonnell Douglas DC-10 Avionics

CONTINENTAL AIRLINES

Certificate of Training

Be it known that

ROBERT C. WITBECK

has successfully completed

B727 AVIONICS/ELECTRICAL

on this FIRST *day of* MARCH *nineteen*

hundred and NINETY-ONE

Instructor
Maintenance Training

Manager
Maintenance Training

Boeing 727 Avionics/Electrical

CONTINENTAL AIRLINES

Certificate of Training

Be it known that

ROBERT C. WITBECK

has successfully completed

B747 ELECT/AVIONICS

on this 26TH *day of* MAY *nineteen*

hundred and 88

Instructor
Maintenance Training

Manager
Maintenance Training

Boeing 747 Electrical/Avionics

Continental

Certificate of Training

Be it known that

Robert C. Witbeck

has successfully completed

B737-100/200/300/500 Airframe & Powerplant Course (80 Hours)

on this 2nd day of September nineteen

hundred and Ninety four

Instructor
Maintenance Training

Manager
Maintenance Training

Boeing 737-100/200/300/500 Airframe and Powerplant Course

Continental

Certificate of Training

Be it known that

Robert C Witbeck

has successfully completed

B 737-300 Avionics / Electrical Course

on this 23rd day of July nineteen

hundred and Ninety Three

Instructor
Maintenance Training

Manager
Maintenance Training

Boeing 737–300 Avionics/Electrical Course

6

DEVELOPING GREAT MENTORS

This was an area that I would have never considered. While working your shift, you will experience long periods of downtime. AKA *"feast or famine,"* either you're busy as hell or bored as hell. As a young man full of curiosity, I found myself learning about people's personal experiences in such a way that I could never have imagined. Ranging in ages from the high 60s down close to my age, my co-workers made me look at areas that I needed. Many were ex-military, and few were still enlisted. Other ways of gaining wealth were proven by viewing the individual face-to-face. Countless millionaires have blossomed from this career. Important things like being told how important your credit score is. Many had side businesses such as rental property, laundry mats, restaurants, and retail stores, to name a few.

I have been exposed to many mentors who were from other cultures and countries, such as the Philippines, Vietnam, Taiwan, China, Saudi Arabia, Jordan, Egypt, Ethiopia, India, and Mexico, to name a few. I got a bird's-eye perspective on many countries that you don't find in the media.

7

TRAVEL BENEFITS

Every company you work for has its perks, such as food discounts, clothing discounts, etc. But to fly FREE (excluding taxes) almost anywhere in the freaking world! Sure it's standby or as we call it *"non-revenue"* because the company doesn't make any money off of that seat that you are sitting in. In addition to flight passes, companies offer airline employee discounts on hotels, car rentals, and many other travel or non-travel-related discounts. I've saved tens of thousands of dollars through the years. One year between Christmas and New Year's, my wife, I, and my 2 daughters went to Honolulu for a full week, including hotel discounts. To top it off, when you retire, you receive a retirement badge which includes lifetime flight benefits. How cool is that!

8

UNIONS

As the boom of industrialization prospered in the United States along with many other countries, labor became the critical factor in the growth process. The first existing union intervention that showed successful progress was the 1877 Granite Cutters' 1st Health Plan. Steel producers, auto makers, coal mining, railroads, and many large and small corporations needed labor badly. In the beginning, there was not much focus on the working conditions of the laborers. Many deaths were directly attributed to these working conditions. Unions came into existence to combat poor working conditions. Today, we take so much for granted when we start a new job. 8-hour workday, 40-hour work week, sick pay, medical and dental care, equal pay, pay raises, retirement pay, etc. Well, NONE OF THAT EXISTED IN THE BEGINNING! It was just the opposite of the above, as such forced work hours, no sick pay, no medical or dental care, unequal pay, no pay raises, no retirement, and so on. Oh, by the way, if it was reported that you were complaining about the work conditions, you got terminated and immediately replaced. The union changed all of that through countless years of negotiation, which later became state requirements. As we use those 18-wheeled trucks that roll across our highways today, we don't think much of them. Some of us don't even think about how this type of transport even started. Before there were trucks, there were horses and buggies called Teamsters.

In the labor industry, No Color Line policies had to be implemented. Many companies would pay white workers more for the same work description compared to African-Americans and other minority workers. Labor unions were instrumental in creating fair wage practices.

Why do some companies have labor unions for their hourly workers, and some don't?

The companies that tend to have more compassion for all of their employees are those where unions don't exist. However, the most common reason why operators' labor unions exist is that they want to have a direct relationship with their staff and workers. It also costs them more money. Research shows that the growth of union jobs correlates with higher wages for the lowest-paid workers.

I was first introduced to labor unions at a company called Executive Jet Aviation, Inc. in the early '80s. It was pretty cut and dry. I was told that you have to join the union, and they will deduct an initiation fee and monthly dues out of my paycheck.

Ironically, my dad told me a story about my great-grandfather, who was a big union man back in Pennsylvania. During a strike at the steel plant, violence broke out, and he was indicted for murder. According to a book that was written, the charges were eventually dropped. The Homestead Strike of 1892 is still in print today, and my great-grandfather was actually mentioned in the book! Why is it still in print? This strike was so violent that the federal government had to get involved and make changes so lives would not be lost again. Some colleges and universities still assign this publication for students to read.

9

LIFE AS AN AIRCRAFT MAINTENANCE SHOP STEWARD

The reason why I became a shop steward is that I like to help people. However, it's not for everybody. It can be a thankless job. In some cases, the tech that you are representing takes you for granted, not really realizing that we don't get paid. We volunteer our personal time on and off the job to research grievances in order to win his/her case. This unique training while learning contract language felt great to belong to a brotherhood. It's kind of like an attorney/public defender. Working with management in an unusual way. We are trained to understand that our position is equal to that of those we speak to when it comes to a union-related issue. From supervisor to Senior Director. It is a highly respected position on the job. Some shop stewards are promoted to management positions.

During contract negotiations, many of the techs wanted it explained how that sort of thing played out. I always liked to use the *"Bowl of Fruit"* metaphor. During negotiations, management and the union have a bowl of fruit in front of them. Each fruit type represents a compensation, for example, pay raises or benefits, and how much the company is willing to budget. Yes, management has a budget that they are supposed to stay within. Well, this bowl of fruit slides back and forth across the table, whereas fruits are removed for others and then given back to the union, and so on.

Contract negotiations break down into two main categories: Economic and non-economic issues, known as Articles. For example, economic issues deal with wages, benefits, and retirement, which cost the company the most money. Non-economic issues, on the other hand, cover non-money issues like work conditions, seniority provisions, and safety standards. Non-economic Articles are usually negotiated first because the economic articles take most of the time to ratify. As a mechanic, I strongly suggest you read the WHOLE tentative agreement before voting on it. I usually never vote positively on the one first handed to me.

Some contract negotiations can last for several months or several years.

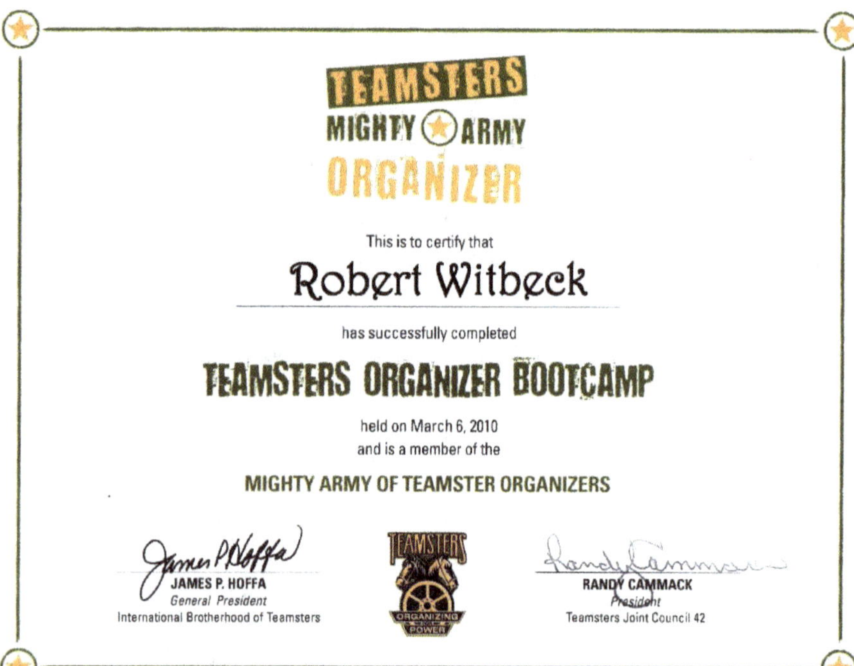

Certificate of Completion

This award is presented to

Robert Witbeck

For successfully completing all required coursework and training for
Teamsters Continental & ExpressJet Airlines
Stewards Seminar

James P. Hoffa
James P. Hoffa
General President

July 11, 2003
Date

Certificate of Completion

Is hereby granted to

Robert C. Witbeck

For successfully completing the

International Brotherhood of Teamsters
Stewards Training Seminar

May 29-30, 2008
Teamsters Local Union No. 986
South El Monte, California

James P. Hoffa
General President

Chris Griswold
Local Union Secretary-Treasurer

10

AAH! THE OVERTIME PAY $$$

Overtime pay in this career is known as a **"Silent Gold Mine."** Most aircraft maintenance operations, especially those of major airlines, can't operate without it. Overtime saves the company money in the long run. Why? For the periods of time that it is offered, the currently staffed techs keep the company from hiring more techs, which includes the more costly benefits they have to pay and train a new hire. It's a win-win for the company and the techs.

During my employment, our latest contract paid us 1 ½ times and double time after completion of our normal shift. On days off, double time is paid for the full shift. Holiday pay (if you choose to work) can be even more. In the course of a year, a tech can easily make more than a supervisor and even, in some cases, shift managers and directors. When working lots of overtime, always review your pay stub. There is a flip side to the above. Your income taxes are proportionate to your earnings. Meaning, Uncle Sam will get a bigger cut. In addition, once these big paychecks are consistent, it can make your budget go out of control. Credit cards can get maxed out, along with other things like fancy car payments. Once the company decides to shut the overtime down, what are you going to do? In order to combat this situation, PAY CASH for things as much as possible. The next thing is safety and health. Putting in many hours can eventually take a toll on your mind and body. Work accidents (sometimes fatal) tend to increase due to mental and physical fatigue. Too many hours at work can affect your judgment and reflexes. Studies show that jobs with an overtime schedule are associated with a 61% higher injury rate. If a job has workers put in 12 hours or more daily, they're at a 37% higher risk of injury. Workers who clock in 60 hours each week are 23% more likely to have an accident.

And lastly, your social life can be highly affected, especially if you are married. Many aviation jobs that operate 24/7 are known as *"The Wicked Mistress."* She's always there for you as long as you are.

11

DEALING WITH ADVERSITY DURING YOUR AVIATION CAREER

An aircraft technician is one of the highest-paying blue-collar jobs. Along with this position comes a large degree of responsibility. Once you sign your name in a logbook, release an aircraft for service, or sign a document, people's lives are in your hands. It starts with you because you are the player. The Lead will be your first line of contact, reporting the status of your assignment. Leads are hourly workers like you. Most of them assist you in getting the assignment done, such as ordering parts and communicating with the supervisor. While your job is dealing with the aircraft, they are dealing with people. Sometimes this is where the problems start. Pressure from upper management can become overwhelming to these guys, which can flow down to you. From my experience, what worked for me was to never make the job your problem. Even though it may not be easy, just think of yourself as a person assigned to help the company with its problem. I always explained the fact that my problems start when I leave at the end of the shift and deal with family and financial matters.

You will work with aircraft maintenance inspectors. Inspectors are paid hourly; however, they are under a completely different technical operations division called Quality Assurance.

Most inspectors are ex-techs with good reading skills. Some inspectors are promoted with very little maintenance experience, and some are very experienced. Some can be extremely picky about what they want you to do, and some are not so picky. Either way, in order to get your job completed, you need them. My success with these gentlemen was just to relax and do what they want, whether you like it or not.

Federal Aviation Administration (FAA) inspectors have the right to enter any job site and check licenses, paperwork, procedures, and techniques of current work. They are kind of like police officers. They might ask you to do a walk-through of your assignment step by step while asking key questions. Please don't lie to them because they are trained to catch you in one.

Many airlines employ a full staff of aircraft engineers. During aircraft modifications, engineers will come to the floor to assist with a project in order for it to flow smoothly, so that if and when a problem with the drawings arises. Just remember, aircraft engineers are not required to be licensed and do not sign anything off regarding the safety of the aircraft. That falls back on you as the responsible tech.

Air and taxi Return issues are situations when an aircraft has been released to fly, but the pilots notice something abnormal. This can become very stressful for everyone. It's like sticking a screwdriver in a machine with many gears. Every person involved with that particular aircraft is initially involved. That includes the FAA because they want to know why. There are many reasons in which an aircraft has to return to the gate. Many times, it's a maintenance problem, or the crew will blame it on maintenance. Whatever the case may be, tension will be high because now you have a plane full of passengers and cargo that's delayed. If it's the plane you were assigned to, it's time to keep a cool head, no matter what's going on around you so it can get flying again. There may come a time when you will deem it safe to ground the plane based on the time and what's involved to fix it.

Damaging an aircraft or maintenance accidents WILL happen during your career. Aircraft during towing, engine changes, electric shock, movement of flight controls are just a few causes of these types of incidents. Worker Complacency is a guiding factor in accidents on airplanes. Overconfidence, shortcuts, lack of communication, and concentration are just a few reasons why they happen. If you personally caused the accident, I suggest taking the hit. Management will have a fact-finding meeting to determine if there will be discipline and or a urine test. I recommend having union representation during this situation. As they say, honesty is the best policy. Making mistakes is part of your career. You gain experience that way, and besides, you're way too valuable and trained for the company to just fire you.

There will come a time in your career when your company will have layoffs and staff reductions. It usually happens when a company has not been showing profits for a long period of time. If you are at the bottom of the seniority list, you go first. It's always good to financially prepare for that time to come.

On the corporate side, you will have to deal with *"corporate trends."* These are ideas that CEOs come up with to save money, improve efficiency (such as AI), or help the morale of the workforce. From my perspective, some work and some don't.

One of the worst corporate trends I've witnessed in my career was the Employee Stock Ownership Plan (ESOP). According to a Harvard Business Review, 8% terminated their pension plan to form ESOPs. Around 40% of all ESOP companies have at least one other pension plan. Around 73% of ESOP companies improved employee work performance after the plan was set up. But here's the catch: when a company files for bankruptcy, this will throw the plan into a horrifying downspin into the hands of some bankruptcy judge. The poor workforce can lose all that was in their plan with no pension at all. Please be aware of this.

12

YOUR HAND TOOLS, COMPANY HAND TOOL & TEST EQUIPMENT

Hand tools are how you make your money. Leaving them on an aircraft in an unsafe place can lead to disaster. I wouldn't initial or put my name on them. Buy good-quality tools. Low-quality tools can actually be unsafe due to low-quality workmanship, such as poor tolerances and finishes. Purchase tools with a reputable warranty, such as Craftsman or Snap-On. Buy only what you need. Many companies issue hand tools in their tool room. Inquire first. I'll get into that later. Keep track of your tools and who you lend them to. Make sure the borrower returns them to you. If you find yourself borrowing a tool more than twice, it's time to purchase your own. I can become very annoying to your co-worker when he realizes that you don't want to invest in your own tools. Company-provided tools, test equipment, and supplies are an extremely vital and important department in technical operations. You will be introduced to hundreds of different types of equipment in order to do your job. Tool rooms are 24/7 and are regulated by the FAA to the highest standards. There are literally thousands of tools and test equipment required in order to safely keep an aircraft in the air. Many require regular calibration dates, such as torque wrenches, on a routine basis. It's your responsibility to check these calibration stickers before you use the tool in an aircraft. When the time comes when you have to perform a work task card on your assigned aircraft, and a piece of equipment is called out, it must be available and calibrated. If not, you can't do the job. The Tool Crib, as some call it, has many other miscellaneous items and functions. Environmental and hazardous materials (HAZMAT) are carefully stored there. Sealants, lubricants, and sprays are maintained and regulated by Shelf-Life Dates. In our paperless society of today, many companies have issued personal iPads. This tool has become a mainstay in the industry due to its multi-functional abilities.

13

PROMOTIONS AND JOB CHANGES

As an entry-level tech, you will be exposed to many career opportunities. They may require certain amounts of experience and training. In-house job openings are posted constantly and are listed on the company website. Outside openings and promotions are a big plus in this technical career. Even the FAA hires and trains techs as inspectors. Smaller operators hire techs, especially with airline experience on the resume.

14

TECHNICAL SKILLS LISTED UNDER THE AIRFRAME & POWERPLANT POSITION (TO NAME A FEW)

Flight Line: Live overnight aircraft

Heavy Check: Deep maintenance check, usually a week or more

Line Sheetmetal: Live overnight aircraft

Heavy Sheetmetal (structures): Deep maintenance, usually a week or more

Heavy Engine Overhaul: Complete teardown

Engine Build Up (EBU): Partial tear-down, mostly outer components

Aircraft Instrument Overhaul: Mechanical and electronic in the cockpit

Wire Harness Buildup

Auxiliary Power Unit (APU) Overhaul: Complete teardown

Test Cell: Final step engine run before making serviceable

Aircraft Interior Repair (AIR): Interior components of the cabin

Avionics Line: Troubleshoot and repair electrical and electronic components

Heavy Avionics: Deep wire and system modifications, usually a week or more

Landing Gear Overhaul: Struts, wheel/tire, and brakes

Flight Simulator: Troubleshoot, repair, and replace components

Rotary Wing (helicopter): Engine and airframe

Non-Aviation

Disney Theme Parks

Amusement Parks

Motor Cycles

Medical Equipment

Semi-trucks (sheet metal)

Robotics

15

SAFETY

In the course of your training, safety will be constantly stressed. You must learn and respect the dangers in and around the aircraft. Aircraft maintenance accidents can range from a minor bump or cut to severe injury and death. **OSHA** had recorded more than 30 severe injuries to techs over the last seven years due to falls from various heights, falling off ladders and or improper use are the cause of several accidents. In order for an aircraft's flight control to move, it takes 3,000 psi or so. So, once one of your limbs gets caught between a flight control during movement, it can crush you like an orange. Two-way communication has proven to be very effective during these types of ground procedures.

Case in Point

One of many fluids we use on the aircraft is *"Skydrol."* It has been scientifically proven to handle the high temperatures and pressures that large aircraft require. However, it is not human flesh-friendly, especially if it gets in your eyes. One evening, one of my co-workers got it in his eyes, and he literally went ballistic. Fortunately, there was some milk in the breakroom refrigerator. I immediately administered it directly in his eye, which lifts this chemical out for instant relief. He always reminded me of the quick and instant relief I gave him that evening.

16

PAY AND BENEFITS (MAJOR AIRLINES)

When I first started my career with a major airline, the old timers in the mid-80s would say, *"We started at $3.19/hour."* However, they left out the fact that the house they are sitting in at the moment costs $15,000 to $20,000! Due to inflation and airline ticket pricing, Techs are topping off at around $60/hr. In some cities, at that wage, you still can't afford to buy a house unless it's 80+ miles away. Obviously wages are important but company benefits hold the same weight. Medical and dental benefits have a large impact on your life when the need arises for you and your family. If you are married and your wife has benefits, you can always use either one instead, which can save you money. Additional benefits include 401(k) company match, paid time off, sick leave, leave of absence (LOA), sick relative leave, death of a relative, and maternity leave. Currently, many companies offer gender friendly benefits. Some cities offer recreational benefits such as ski clubs, fishing clubs, and bowling teams, to name a few.

17

LGBTQ FRIENDLY

Airlines, along with many other companies, are offering better benefits for this community than ever before. Not only is *"spouse,"* but *"companion"* is written in union contracts and company policy manuals. *"Fair and equal," "Don't ask, don't tell"* are now a mainstay. NGPA (National Gay Pilots Association) is now airline-sponsored.

18

SHIFT WORK

Shift work is such a broad title for employers. Days, swings, late swings, graveyard or graves are a part of life that we have grown accustomed to since we can remember. Even as far back as our great-grandparents, this work ethic has been around. However, this concept of work has not always been in existence.

In 1933, a bill was passed and supported by President Franklin D. Roosevelt to reduce the standard workweek to only 30 hours. American slaves generally worked 10-16 hours a day, 6 days a week. When slavery ended, the black workweek fell by 26 to 35%. In the 1830s, workers in manufacturing were at the job around 70 hours a week. By the 1890s, the 60-hour work week came along with labor unions. The Ford Motor Company, with CEO Henry Ford, instituted a 6-day 40-hour work week for male factory workers in 1914, according to history.com. And finally, in 1926, a five-day, 40-hour work week. You can give Mr. Ford credit for arguing that employees were more productive in fewer hours.

For techs, general aviation is usually a day shift, and airlines are 24/7. With an airline, you must be prepared to work all shifts. In the course of my training, we were introduced to the Circadian Rhythm. This concept of easily focusing on the body's internal clock explains why working the night shift is problematic. Your health and diet also play an important part in nights due to the fact that it goes against the grain of society. When it comes to nights and swing shift, there are pros and cons. The pros: I raised my family on nights due to the flexible, free daytime hours when it comes to school activities and sports for the kids. Some people maintain a side business such as rental property, laundry mats, and retail stores. You actually save money because you don't go out as much during your work week. I worked the 4-day work week from 1995 to 2021. Many companies in countries such as Australia, Canada, and Germany have implemented the 4-day work week. It saves on auto gas by only working 16 days a month. Commuters and carpoolers love it too for the same reasons.

The cons are sleep deprivation due to irregular sleep habits which leads to difficulty with concentration and focusing in the workplace. It wreaks havoc on your immune system, which lowers your resistance to fight off viruses. Also, without enough sleep, you can become irritable and snappy around your loved ones if you're not careful. When it comes to your social life, it sucks because most of the world is in bed while you are at work. When I met my wife, I worked nights, and she never really liked it.

19

THE WEATHER FACTOR

Obviously, airplanes have to be outside in the elements. Techs, along with everybody else, have to deal with it. Machinery and cold weather don't get along. That includes the aircraft and ground support equipment (GSE). When it gets in single-digit temperatures, we would leave the equipment running due to the fact that it might not start up. The internal combustion engine gets congested, making it hard to crank. However, electric vehicles tend to be more reliable. Lithium-ion batteries thrive in cold weather over lead-acid batteries. Lead acid batteries' operating temperature is around 77° F, and decreases their efficiency by 10% every 10-degree drop. On the other hand, the lithium battery can operate from -4° F to 131° F and keeps the same power easily, doing a full crank shift. Removing and replacing aircraft tires and brakes is labor-intensive and pretty routine. Airlines block these items more heavily in southern and western states, where the climate is more maintenance-friendly. If you are a little more fortunate, you might be able to work in a heated aircraft hangar. Some hangars have heated floors, whereas the heat is generated under the concrete with hot water piping. With that said, many techs will have to work in a cold climate at one time or another.

Case in Point

Back in the 80s, I was assigned to remove and replace an electric fuel boost pump in the wing of a Lockheed L-1011. The temperature was around 15° F on the flight line of Indianapolis Int'l Airport. This particular pump is actually a *"quick-disconnect"* style unit. However, for some reason, the new one wouldn't go in. I tried several times with jet fuel running down my arm to install this fuel pump. One in our Leads suggested removing the rubber *"O-Ring"* seals from the pump and bringing it into the maintenance office. We dumped seals of a cup of hot water, brought them outside, and put the back on the pump right away. Like magic, the pump slipped right in and locked!

20

I FOUND MY NICHE

I worked 7 years as an Airframe & Powerplant (A&P) tech and 35 years as an Avionics tech. A&P is mostly Remove and Replace (R&R) and routine jobs such as oil changes, lubrication, tires, and brakes. Once I switched over to avionics, I was introduced to a whole new world called troubleshooting, which I fell in love with. Diagnosing problems, no matter how long it took, seemed to make the shift go by quickly. Along with job satisfaction, I was highly respected by co-workers and management. On occasion, some aircraft may fly around for weeks with a chronic problem. Your assignment is to fix it. If you are successful, you are the man! As an avionics tech, you really have to learn how each system works in order to troubleshoot it. You will have to dive deeply into wiring diagrams, schematics, and maintenance manuals. On test flights, pilots preferred one of us to go. On many modification projects, we worked closely with engineering.

The downside of this cool skill is that you can get ELECTICUTED. I've been there and done that several times. I totally understand why guys don't want to do it, and I don't blame them. My rule of thumb is to respect electricity and follow established safety procedures; you will not become a statistic. Twenty-eight volts DC feels like a pin prick, and 115-volt AC about a 12-volt car spark plug. If you are working on a ladder, you will fall off. If you are working behind a major electrical panel, you will *black out.* I am a survivor.

Oh, while we are on the subject, never do electrical work on an aircraft while it's wet or in the rain. Water is an excellent conductor.

57

21

CHARLES E. TAYLOR (1868-1956) "THE FIRST AIRPLANE MECHANIC."

We all have to pay homage to the first. From a pig farmer to *"Mechanician."* Mr. Taylor built bicycles for the Wright brothers and owned a machine shop. When the Wright Brothers needed an engine for the Kittyhawk, no company would build just one engine. Charles said, *"I will build it."* He built the engine from scratch in 6 weeks. When their planes crashed, Charles rebuilt them. There are other notable vintage techs that I will mention later in this book.

22

COMPANY-PROVIDED HAND TOOLS, EQUIPMENT, AND SUPPLIES

There are literally thousands of hand tools, equipment & supplies to make an aircraft safe. Many aircraft parts are too heavy for a man to lift, which requires special lift tools or test equipment in order to simulate a flight condition on the ground. Each make and model requires its own tools and equipment. For example, an Engine Change Kit for a Boeing 767 and 787 may differ considerably. Many tools, such as torque wrenches and avionics test equipment, require periodic calibration and have to be removed from service and returned with a new sticker and the next due date. A shelf life is put on sealants, adhesives, tapes, etc., so they must be pulled off the shelf when they expire. These are items that a tech must be aware of when applying and working on an aircraft. Hazardous Materials (HAZMAT) are made readily available, such as lubricants, aerosols, solvents, etc., that can't be disposed of in regular trash due to environmental restrictions.

Techs receive training on handling HAZMAT. One of the most nifty tools that was recently provided by our technical operations department was the iPad! It actually has been long overdue because an item of this nature has to be approved by the F.A.A. When I was first hired in this career field, I was told to prepare for filling out a lot of forms and documents. The iPad reduces a large majority of paperwork from the past. You can quickly download the manuals for each plane in seconds, from any location, which makes your job easier.

So, where do I get all this stuff from at my place of work? Well, some companies call it the Tool Room or Tool Crib. Just about every maintenance station in the system has a department of this nature. The larger tool rooms ship and receive tools and equipment all over the world when needed and operate 24/7 with a full staff of attendants. With an airline, you may find yourself making countless trips courtesy to this department, in order to complete your maintenance tasks.

23

AIRCRAFT PARTS

Obviously, aircraft parts are expensive. An electronic box (black box) can range from $10,000 to $100,000+. A commercial jet engine with its extreme thrust and high-altitude capability is in a price range between $5 and $50 million, depending on the size and mission requirements. Remember, most commercial jets have at least 2 engines!

It's estimated that major legacy airlines' parts inventory, around $1.5-$2 billion of inventory, turns over at fewer than 1.7 times per year.

I will not venture into the particulars of this mass department. We want to cover what applies to you as a tech. Once you install a part on the aircraft, it's your responsibility.

The IPC (Illustrated Part Catalog) will help you find the correct part for each particular aircraft. The IPC is the most important manual you will use and the most regularly updated. According to staff aeronautics engineers, *"It's your Bible."*

In the field, you will notice many of the expensive parts called *"rotables"* are not readily available at your location. In some cases, due to high state inventory taxes on parts such as hydraulic pumps, electronic boxes, fuel valves, etc., they are stored in locations where there is low or no inventory tax. We've always joked around when seeing some of the prices of aircraft parts and said, *"We're in the wrong part of the business."*

Case in Point

In the 80s, at an FBO, while troubleshooting a steering problem on a 20 Series Learjet, I had to remove the whole nose gear assembly. After fabricating a *"patch harness,"* I realized that the steering servo unit was bad. I removed it and handed it to my maintenance manager to have it overhauled. He brought it back to me and said it was fixed. I asked him, *"Where's the serviceable tag?"* Since he couldn't produce one, I refused to install it in the plane. Why is that tag so important? In the event of an accident, the FAA will want to know who actually repaired that particular component and where they were certified to do so.

In the 90s, as a union steward, I was called out to represent a tech about an incident. The CAA (Civil Aeronautics Authority) boarded a McDonnell Douglas DC-10 for a spot inspection. They found some POB (Portable Oxygen Bottles) with expired serviceable tags. How do you trace those POBs back to this tech? It's actually pretty simple with good records. During the line overnight check or overhauls, a work card was signed off by him stating that the units were serviceable. Acting as his representative, I quickly challenged management that those bottles could have been swapped out due to the easy access location. Fortunately, the tech was cleared.

One night, I was assigned to address a problem on a Boeing 757-200. Upon departure at the terminal, the flight crew noticed *"smoke in the passenger cabin."* The plane was grounded. Upon investigation, we found the upper ceiling light assembly severely burned. I immediately ordered the complete assembly and found that we had none in stock. My maintenance foremen and technical support decided that they would have me salvage the light assembly with various electrical parts, sandpaper, and spray paint, and send the aircraft on its way. When presented with this approach, I politely made the decision to await a new or serviceable part ordered from stock. Why? Whenever an aircraft is pulled from the gate on a scheduled flight for a maintenance problem, the FAA is automatically notified. My decision eliminated me from getting involved in any part installation that had questionable serviceability.

24

QUALITY CONTROL (QC)

In technical operations, this department has its own separate organizational chart. With this system in place, it satisfies the FAA's safety requirements. Maintenance management has no jurisdiction over decisions made by QC regarding an aircraft issue.

With good reading skills, a tech can be promoted to an inspector with a huge raise in pay. A large part of your job will be working with inspectors. In many cases, you will need an inspector to *"buy off"* your work in order to finalize your job. All inspectors are not the same. Some are seasoned with decades of hands-on experience, and some have the minimum experience to qualify for the position. Techs get into arguments with these guys because they need them to buy off their work. I've always found it better to submit to them and do what they ask. Once you develop their trust, it will be better the next time. Remember, inspectors can get in even deeper trouble with the FAA than you if they screw up.

I have always had a deep respect for this department because QC management always confidently stands by their inspectors if an aircraft is grounded.

25

ENGINEERING

Most large airlines have a staff of engineers. Their department is subdivided into areas like structures, propulsion (engines), electrical, avionics, etc. They may come to the floor and assist in many aircraft modifications. Your relationship with them will involve performing the work in the form of drawings and step-by-step instructions. Engineering Authorizations (EAs) are modifications of a smaller level of complexity. These documents will come down from their department with no engineer present. Never start an EA without a hard copy in hand. Many EAs come with a parts list or a parts kit. Always make an inventory of all parts needed. If there are parts missing, you can't start the modification. Management may be pressured to get an EA done quickly. Just remember to pace yourself. Finally, engineers are not FAA-licensed technicians. It is still your responsibility to release an airworthy plane after a modification has been completed.

26

FLIGHT SIMULATOR TECHNICIAN

Flight simulators came into existence in the 1920s and 30s. The best known at this time was the Link Trainer designed by Edwin Link Jr. in Binghamton, New York. This innovative design with weather features included was patented in 1929. Mr. Link's invention didn't catch on for several years. By the mid-1930s, the United States Army Air Force (USAAF) showed interest, and after many pilots were killed due to weather reasons. Today, flight simulators are a thriving industry with many aircraft types. Their design is so precise that pilots say it is more difficult to fly than the actual plane. NASA's Space Shuttle has its own simulator.

Today, the flight simulator is a critical tool for pilots to log flight hours and, in turn, save hundreds of thousands of dollars in fuel and wear and tear on the planes. They have the ability to select any airport in the world in order to land and take off.

A flight simulator technician usually has a higher salary. It requires extensive avionics training and experience to maintain these units.

Case in Point

In the late 1980s, I had an opportunity to fly on an Airbus A-300 flight simulator. As I rolled out, full throttle, took off, and gained altitude, my instructor tapped me on the shoulder and pointed at the temperature gauges on the engines. Both engines were in an over-temperature condition (redline) because I failed to pull the throttles back in time after take-off. What a lesson!

There is one switch that the A-300 Airbus flight simulator has that the actual aircraft doesn't have, and that's *"Crash Override."*

27

MAINTENANCE CONTROL

Maintenance control is part of the aircraft technical operations (Tech-Ops) department in most airlines. Their facilities are usually in one location with a full staff of maintenance, controllers, and management. This department runs 24/7 with no exceptions. What you and maintenance control have in common is the Minimum Equipment List (MEL). Each aircraft has its own list. When a problem arises that will cause an aircraft to be grounded, it will be your job to work with them in order to get the plane out on time and safe in accordance with the MEL. Can an airplane fly with only one altimeter? The MEL will let you know if it's possible or not. This group can get you out of lots of binds at the gate when you need them most. Maintenance controller is another promotional opportunity for techs.

28

AIRCRAFT MAINTENANCE TECHNICAL SUPPORT

Maintenance technical support staffing has been in existence for over forty years. I call them *"Technicians with a Tie"* as part of Maintenance Control. These are highly experienced individuals with extensive training on many types of aircraft. They face challenges that require electrical, electronic, and mechanical skills. Tech support staff work directly on the aircraft with technicians. When an aircraft has a continuous malfunction for a long period of time, it is called a *"chronic."* Tech support staff and techs work on this problem non-stop until it's fixed. Technical Support staff offices are usually located at large maintenance bases where they have access to techs, tools, and test equipment needed to perform their job. At shift change, tech support staff act as an excellent tie-in. One of the most valuable assets that tech support has is its direct link with several aircraft manufacturers. Vital up-to-date aircraft fleet problems, defective parts, modifications, bulletins, and many other issues are needed to keep our fleet in the air.

I've always enjoyed working with our technical support staff. These positions are usually filled by sharp, young, and motivated technicians.

29

COMPANY BANKRUPTCIES

When an individual or family files for bankruptcy, it can be an emotional and embarrassing experience. When a company files, it's nothing more than a business decision. U.S. Corporate bankruptcies have been on the rise for over a decade now, according to S&P Global Market Intelligence data. Airlines have been filing for bankruptcy protection since the early 1980s. Airline deregulation by the US government had a significant effect on this industry. Some operators use these filings as a handy tool to tame huge labor disputes.

As a technician, your wallet will let you know when your company files for bankruptcy.

Even the news media will find out before you. In my company, some techs didn't find out until their own bank refused to deposit their payroll check. Now that sucks! There are many reasons why bankruptcies are filed, such as a slow economy, recession, high unemployment, mismanagement, etc. Airlines operate at such a small profit margin that it just takes the slightest glitch in the economy for it to take a hit. Unfortunately, layoffs, and furloughs are part of this career. There is really nothing you can do about it except go with the flow. I've experienced 2 company bankruptcies in my career. I was fortunate at the time to have enough seniority to keep my job; unfortunately, many management positions, which have no bargaining contracts, end up being part of the *"slaughterhouse"* of job losses. For safety reasons, the FAA requires a minimum number of techs per aircraft to operate a carrier.

R.C. Witbeck (Acetech)

the FAA requires a minimum number of techs per aircraft to operate a carrier.

30

COMPANY MERGERS AND ACQUISITIONS (M&AS)

M&As go back to the beginning of man's dealings with each other. However, in the modern era, the 1st mergers started in the early 1880s. Term mergers and acquisitions refer to the consolidation of companies or major assets through financial transactions between companies. Throughout history, merger activity went in waves due to factors such as the economy, regulatory changes, and technological shocks. Up until 2007, M&As amounted to hundreds of billions of dollars. The ultimate goal of an M&A is to benefit both companies.

My company suffered many failed attempts to merge. Finally, the perfect fit arrived. After it was all said and done, it took around 10 years. Ours consisted of waves of layoffs, disorganization, and mismanagement. I won't get into the details of how M&As are categorized. In my company, it was considered non-hostile, *"Big Fish Eat the Little Fish,"* and heavily government-regulated. This is what big corporations do, and we have to live with it. In many cases, some CEO will take all the credit for being the one to get it done. One good thing about our merger is that the US government would not allow our pension fund to be affected.

31

MY FAVORITE SHIFT

In my career, I've worked practically all shifts available, such as days, swing, and nights. Day shift for hourly people usually starts between 6 am and ends at 2:30 pm. It has its pros and cons. Getting up that early sucks, and for some reason, I couldn't get to bed early enough to be rested. On party nights, I usually stayed up, showered, and went straight to work! It's even worse if you have a long commute. All in all, the day shift goes with the grain of society.

Swing shift, swings, or 2nd shift, as some people call it, has an interesting twist. Depending on your lifestyle, it can be a bit challenging or pretty simple. Here we go, this shift usually starts at 2 to 4 pm and ends at around 11pm to midnight. Many times, I found myself watching TV very late, and there are some who play video games. So, there's not much to go anywhere. I kind of slept in until the time for work, unless I had an appointment or something. Occasionally, we would hit the bars after work. By that time, the women are already drunk or relaxed. No big deal, right? If you're single. Now, if you're married with children and don't share the same shift, it can get a little complicated. You might find your spouse juggling between activities with the children and, at the same time, trying to be a loving wife or husband. It's tough, but it can work.

And last but not least, graves, graveyard, or 3rd shift. Graves usually start at 11 p.m. and end at 7 a.m. Many years ago, I had a friend who worked for McDonnell Douglas Aircraft. His company offered an incentive to work nights. You work from midnight to 6 am and get paid for eight hours. Obviously, the most senior guys filled those slots. Some call the night shift *"going against the grain of life."* Now, you have to sleep when everyone else is awake. The gardener, chatting with neighbors, playing children, construction noise, etc. It's tough; however, it has its pros and cons. I just covered some of the cons. Abnormal sleep habits affect your mind and body after long periods of time. As mentioned earlier, Circadian Rhythms are physical, mental, and behavioral changes that follow a 24-hour cycle. These natural processes respond primarily to light and dark and affect most living things, including animals, plants, and microbes. Chronobiology is the study of circadian rhythms. Studies show that by limiting caffeine, alcohol, nicotine, and some medicines, especially close to bedtime, you can manage your exposure to light. When working nights, it's recommended to darken the room and avoid TV screens and electronic devices in order to optimize your rest.

If you are single, Graves is not as bad. On my days off, I found myself *"out-partying"* everyone else who doesn't work your shift. If you are married with children, YOU ARE NOT AT HOME AT NIGHT! Interestingly, lots of things seem to happen at night, such as sick children and a lonely wife. Quality time is needed and valued more.

I kind of found my niche when it comes to shift work. As an incentive to work nights, my company offered a 4-day work week or *"4/10s:"* 4 days on and 3 days off. It just seemed like a win-win for me. Some companies offer 4 10s day shift and/or night shift. 4/10s have great advantages. Many other countries have adapted to this shift for their employees for the following reasons:

1. Improves morale in the workplace

2. Saves gas if you drive to work

3. Improves family life

4. Saves wear and tear on the work vehicle

5. Longer vacation time

I would report to work at 9:30 pm and get off at 7 am. In my later years, I was able to get Friday, Saturday, and Sunday off. I was already on this shift when I met my wife. After I got married, she kind of tolerated it. Flexibility was the key that enabled us to raise our daughters on nights.

The Traffic Factor

As a tech, you won't be working out of your home. For many Americans, commuting to work is part of everyday life. In 2019, the average worker commuted more than 27.6 minutes to work, according to the U.S Census. In some larger metropolitan areas, alternative forms of transportation are available. Bus, train, and carpooling have many advantages, especially cost savings. Fuel, auto maintenance, and insurance can be significantly lower on a routine basis. So, where are we getting at here? Working swings or nights falls perfectly with commuting due to the fact that your commute will go against the normal grain of traffic. There will be less stress, fewer stop-and-go situations, and fewer chances of an accident.

32

I CAN'T HEAR YOU!

Occupational hearing loss can occur when you are exposed to loud noise or ototoxic chemicals while at work. Noise is considered loud (hazardous) when it reaches 85 A-weighted decibels (dBA) or higher. Tinnitus is an annoying buzzing, rushing, or ringing noise in your ears or in your head. Secondly, exposure to certain chemicals can cause damage to different parts of the ear, meaning they are ototoxic. Exposure to ototoxic chemicals can cause hearing loss and make the ears more sensitive to the harmful effects of noise. About 10 million workers are exposed to solvents, and an unknown number are exposed to other ototoxicants. Unfortunately, most hearing loss occurs slowly over time.

Regretfully, aircraft mechanics are exposed to the worst of noise of all occupations in the world. Jet engines emit approximately 140 dB(A), with some jets even hitting 190 dB(A). With that said, you may be assigned to do leak checks and power adjustments next to the engine at idle. Then, the mechanic in the cockpit running the engine will be required to throttle the engine to full power right there on the flight line. I've been there countless times. The aviation industry is totally aware of this work hazard. Most airlines require employees to take hearing tests biannually. These hearing tests are performed by an independent firm providing continuous education on hearing loss prevention, components of the inner ear, and how to install your hearing protection properly.

Hearing Loss Trivia

Why does the left ear seem to always have slightly more hearing loss than the right?

Answer: Most of us drive with the window down, which exposes more direct noise to the left ear.

Can I study for my hearing test? Ha Ha Ha!

Fortunately, in my 42 years of experience, I tried my best to preserve my hearing by wearing the proper protection that the job provided. So far, my hearing is normal.

33

AIRCRAFT MECHANIC (AMT) VS AVIONICS TECHNICIAN

When I'm asked what my profession is, I say *"aircraft tech."* Then I get the second question. What exactly do you do? This tells me that my career is somewhat curious and intriguing to people. It's actually a good question. As mentioned in the previous chapter, the great Charles Taylor was the first aircraft mechanic that we know of here in America. For clarification purposes, there are two major divisions in this profession; civilian and military. I will only cover the civilian side. Just like the human body, an aircraft has many separate systems to make it function. Aircraft companies utilize skills based on need. In general, corporate aviation specialization is less needed. However, airlines tend to use more specialists in order to complete a particular task more efficiently and to minimize delays at the gate. The term *"Mechanic"* and *"Technician"* in the aviation industry is used fairly loosely. Mechanics are usually assigned to more hands-on tasks, such as brake, tire, hydraulic, fuel, flight control, environmental systems, and engine changes, to name a few. In order to perform their task, larger hand tools are required. Technicians, especially avionics technicians, are somewhat specialized and are usually assigned to the electrical and electronic portion of those same systems of the aircraft, utilizing schematics and wiring diagrams.

Their job is usually performed with smaller tools and test equipment used to troubleshoot numerous problems that come up. In many cases, the avionics technician may diagnose a problem with a certain mechanical component that the mechanic is more skilled to replace. Avionics technicians really have to learn how a system works in order to diagnose a problem. In a line maintenance setting where the aircraft are *"live,"* meaning they will be going out within 24 hours, we all work together to get the plane out safely and on time. In my career, I have had the opportunity to work on all of the above assignments and tasks. In addition, there are other highly skilled mechanics and technicians, such as sheet metal, paint, and aircraft interior repair (AIR), who are vital team members. Lastly, there are the *"shops"* that repair and overhaul components of the airplane, such as engines, pumps, electronic boxes, landing gear, etc. Whether independent or in-house, these support shops are also greatly needed to keep the plane flying.

34

THE CARGO FREIGHTERS AND PARCEL CARRIERS

In 1910, the first known air freight shipment on a cargo-only plane took to the skies from Dayton, OH, to Columbus, OH. The model B plane, invented by the famous Wright Brothers, raced against an express train to see which method could deliver a shipment silk the quickest. With a trouble-free flight of less than an hour, the plane won, clearly demonstrating to the world that air freight or sea freight could be a viable shipping option. In 1911, *"Airmail"* first started in the UK and eventually became a large industry in America. Some of us might be too young to remember the famous postal *"Airmail"* stamp for letters. Flying cargo and parcels is operated under a completely different set of FAA FARs (Federal Aviation Regulations). From an aircraft maintenance standpoint and my personal experience, their regulations are not as strict as passenger carrier regulations. One advantage of flying freight and packages is that you don't have to feed or comfort them, and most of all, no complaining.

Case in Point

Once upon a time, there was a young and somewhat cocky Yale economics student born August 11th, 1944, in Marks, Mississippi, who lost his father at the age of 4. As a Marine, he served five plus years as a platoon commander and pilot in Vietnam. While at Yale in 1965, he wrote a term paper about an advanced idea of an overnight-delivery service, observing that society became more automated and computer companies would need to ensure their products were dependable. His college professor wrote, *"The concept is interesting and well-formed."* He received a *"C."* He took that *"C"* paper and launched a company called Federal Express Corporation, and his name is Frederick W. Smith, CEO and founder, aka the *"father of the overnight delivery business."*

In the early 1980s, I worked for an FBO in Louisville, Kentucky. UPS had just launched its overnight service. Their requirement was to assign aircraft techs to marshal the planes while addressing any maintenance issues from the pilots. One night, a Learjet came in. After cargo door opened, there appeared to be 2 automobile transmissions strapped down. I asked the pilot about it, and he said, *"Those two transmissions are on their way to Detroit because they are holding up an automotive assembly line."*

35

OTHER NOTABLE PIONEER AIRCRAFT MECHANICS

As most know, Howard Hughes was one of the great pioneering aviators of the last century. His vision and contribution to this industry are like no other. From designing many aircraft as a top defense contractor to piloting and breaking death-defying speed records, his accomplishments are still used today. However, behind the scenes with Hughes was flight mechanic, helicopter pilot, and engineer George Kruska. He helped build the legendary Spruce Goose seaplane and continued to maintain it all the way until 1992 to oversee the dismantling for shipment from Long Beach Harbor to Oregon.

I must not fail to mention Glenn Odekirk (1905-1987). Hughes met Odekirk on the set of the Hell's Angels movie (1930). His employment by Hughes helped change aviation history with the design and development of the Hughes H-1 Racer (1935). Groundbreaking technologies were developed during the construction process in order to make this landplane obtain a record-breaking speed of 352 mph.

- A relatively new hardware called **flush rivets** left the aluminum skin completely smooth.
- Hydraulically retractable landing gear and tail skid were also features to maximize speed and reduce drag.
- Two wing designs for short or long-distance racing.

- Pratt & Whitney R-1535 twin row 14-cylinder radial engine rated at 700 HP but tuned up to over 1,000 HP.
- Two-bladed constant speed propeller.

Other than the obsolete engine design, all of the above concepts and designs are the standard of today's aircraft. WOW!

The great magician and escape artist Harry Houdini was a pilot and aviator. In 1909, for $5,000 ($178,000 in today's money), he purchased a French Voisin aircraft and hired a full-time mechanic named Antonio Brassac.

Bessie Coleman (1892-1926) was an early American civil aviator. She was the 1st African-American woman and 1st person of self-identified Native American descent to hold a pilot's license. William D. Willis, 24, was her mechanic and publicity agent. Coleman had recently purchased a poorly maintained Curtiss JN-4 (Jenny). While test flying for an upcoming airshow, Coleman and Willis were both killed when the plane unexpectedly went into a dive and crashed.

36

THE NASA SPACE SHUTTLE *ENDEAVOR* AND ITS FINAL MISSION

The Space Shuttle program's duration was from 1981 to 2011. Also known as the Space Transportation System (STS), its cost was US$196 billion. The program was officially cancelled by President G.W. Bush after 135 missions. STS was the world's first reusable spacecraft launched like a rocket, maneuvered in Earth orbit like a spacecraft, and landed like an airplane. This phenomenal space program hosted on board some 3,000 scientific experiments by leading scientists in their field. Science from the space shuttle helped open the Earth's eyes to the cosmos and sister planets. Creating the most detailed topographical map of Earth is one of the discoveries made aboard.

The reason why I wrote this chapter is that I was part of one of the most unique opportunities in my aviation career to be up front and close to the inner workings of this program right before my eyes.

In order for the space shuttle *Endeavor* to reach its final resting place, a lot of preparation had to take place. The City of Los Angeles, FAA, Los Angeles International Airport, United Airlines, The California Science Center, and a few local TV stations, to name a few.

One of our hangars was designated to house the shuttle for 30 days prior to its snail's pace to move to the science center. This was exactly where I worked every day! Bleacher seats, speaker podiums, tables, and a temporary chef's kitchen were provided to accompany special guests, politicians, and VIPs during and after the multiple flybys and landing of the *Endeavor*. Once the special Boeing 747 and the attached shuttle were parked, a series of special trucked-in equipment had to be used to carefully detach and remove the shuttle from the 747 in order to place it on a multi-wheeled, remote-controlled platform. Once secured on the platform, it was moved to her 30-day hotel stay in Hangar Bay 5. Special pieces of protective equipment had to be installed over the rocket boosters. While in the hangar, hundreds of people who were able to get access came to take pictures of the shuttle. Once exiting LAX on October 12th, 2012, a Toyota Tundra advertising stunt was staged prior to its final journey. Intense cooperation between cities and neighborhoods, such as Westchester, Inglewood, and West Los Angeles, had to cut trees, remove signs, reinforce streets with steel plates, and rearrange overhead electrical wiring. According to the Science Center, on its 160-wheel remote carrier, the distance will be a 12-mile 48-hour task at a cost of $12 million.

37

AIRLINE FOOD AND ENTERTAINMENT

Even though the company strictly prohibited techs from eating or drinking catered food off the aircraft, working for a major airline, you are exposed to the delicious foods. In 1st class, seafoods such as smoked salmon, cooked shrimp, lobster mac & cheese, prime steaks, and large bone pork chops. Chef prepared salads and desserts with fine wines, and liqueurs were a unique kind of educational experience.

Aircraft charters were a lucrative income and also provided a fine dining experience. Multiple sports organizations, such as the NBA, NFL, MLB, and NCAA, are frequent flyers based on their season. College teams usually received a really nice "bag meal," usually from a local fast-food establishment. Once an athlete reaches the professional level, the whole dining experience rises to the next level. Lobster tails, filet mignon steaks, scampi shrimp, along with gourmet side dishes and desserts to supply hungry appetites. I noticed that only the Major League Baseball players always stocked plenty of peanut butter and jelly sandwiches on board. And finally, at the pro level, special request is taken individually from each athlete by the staff prior to their flight. If he or she wants special snacks such as Skittles, Pringles, or certain candy bars, their requests will be granted. Is that cool or what?

Entertainment systems (IFE) on aircraft have improved considerably in the last 60 years.

In 1963, Avid Airline Products developed and manufactured the first pneumatic headset used on board the airlines and provided these early systems to Trans World Airlines (TWA). They were simple hollow tubes that produced a *"stethoscope effect"* sound. In 1979, pneumatic headsets were phased out by electronic headsets.

By the late 70s and 80s, cassettes and discs with quick-inert-deck players were introduced along with Sony 3-Gun overhead projectors. With this format, the latest Hollywood movie releases were shown on the aircraft. Today, with Satellite Communications (SATCOM), we can provide on-demand direct streaming with less hardware. IFE systems virtually provide entertainment close to your own couch at home. As an avionics technician, you will be responsible for maintaining IFE systems primarily because of the FAA-approved passenger safety demonstration that is incorporated as part of its media.

Case in Point

FAA inspectors have the right to enter any aircraft maintenance facility as long as they call ahead. Their duties usually entail checking signed-off maintenance documents, viewing live maintenance being performed, checking mechanics' licenses, etc. One night, I got a call from my lead, and he said, *"The FAA guy wants to speak with you."* When I got there, the inspector had the previous paperwork that I had just signed off on. It was a task card for the aircraft IFE system on a Boeing 757. However, I forgot to check off one of the 2 boxes in order to complete the task card. The first box asked if I used a *"cleaning tape"* to clean the tape deck heads. The second box asked if I used a *"swab and isopropyl alcohol"* to clean the tape deck heads. So, I checked the box regarding the latter. So the inspector said, *"Take me to where you keep these items that you used."* While on the way, he asked, *"Describe to me what these items look like."* So, I did and then showed him. Obviously, the inspector was trying to catch me in a lie to see if I actually did the task at all, which ended the investigation. Once again, when it comes to FAA Maintenance Inspectors, honesty is the best policy.

38

THE NEW BREED: BOEING 787 DREAMLINER

To date, the Boeing 787 Dreamliner Series is the most sophisticated jet airliner ever made. It entered into service in 2011. In my 42 years, I have never experienced an aircraft so unique from all the rest! This wide-body aircraft is manufactured and developed by Boeing Commercial Airplanes. The program was on April 26, 2004, with an order of 50 aircraft from All Nippon Airways (ANA). Boeing targeted it to burn 20% less fuel than its predecessor, the Boeing 767, carrying 200 to 300 passengers on point-to-point routes up to 8,500 nautical miles (15,700 km, 9,800 mi). The Dreamliner's propulsion consists of twinjet engines.

General Electric GENX or Rolls-Royce Trent 1000 high-bypass turbo fans. Its fuel efficiency is attributed to the airframe, which is primarily made of composite materials, and makes extensive use of electrical systems. With foreign competition alive and well, Boeing list-priced the Dreamliner as low as $100 million and up to $338 million, depending on the series and what the customer specifically ordered. Being the first to introduce a new innovation of any commercial jet airline company, the 787 has two lithium-ion main aircraft batteries. Like many new innovations, it had its problems. The new batteries encountered problems, causing onboard fires on some aircraft. In January 2013, the FAA grounded all 787s until it approved the revised battery design in April 2013. This was a major financial setback for Boeing Aircraft.

Fortunately, there were no hull losses and zero fatalities regarding this issue.

From a technical standpoint, let's say the Dreamliner is definitely creating a relaxing feeling of *"job security."* I literally had to throw all my prior training out the window when performing any tasks on this aircraft. One of the biggest reasons was that my company was the first US airline to order the plane. Along with being a new breed of aircraft, Boeing indirectly used us as an extension of their own technical support. This wide-body airliner is literally all software-driven. In the beginning, some software uploads and downloads would take a full 8-hour shift to complete. From my experience, there were no shortcuts of any kind. If you didn't follow the manuals tediously step-by-step, you will end up having to start all over again. Even something as simple as an electric cargo roller unit can't work unless it is properly loaded with software after installation. Something as simple as a routine tire change requires a long list of deactivation steps in order to prevent multiple maintenance messages in the cockpit after reinstallation of the new tire. Most commercial airliners have over 300 circuit breakers in the cockpit alone, with hundreds more situated all over the airplane. Just like in your home, they prevent a short circuit, causing a fire. Shockingly, the Dreamliner has hardly any located in her cockpit! So where are all the cockpit circuit breakers now? There are two permanent electronic computer mice located at the captain's and co-pilot's control pedestal. You locate the circuit breaker pertaining to the system you are working on the LED screen in front of you. Once you find it, you activate or deactivate, and ID tag it with your name virtually. Prior aircraft used forced air in order to keep electronic boxes cool. The '87 had to step it up to another level by encasing some electronic boxes with anti-freeze coolant that need to be serviced prior to installation, which demands even more cooling. As mentioned above, there are two lithium-ion batteries unique to this airplane. As we all know, with our cellphones, lithium-ion batteries can sometimes overheat. Boeing was able to tackle this problem quickly by encasing thick stainless-steel boxes around each battery. With this ingenious modification, any fluid or gases will safely be controlled and expelled overboard. On a battery replacement, there are approximately 50 small bolts and nuts to remove the top from each encased unit. Dreamliners don't have those nuisance and sticky window shades. They just dim electronically by the touch of a button. This aircraft fits perfectly with the tech-savvy mechanics of today.

39.

PIONEERS OF FLIGHT

In the beginnings of American aviation, many young, brave, and enthusiastic pilots lost their lives. Whether it was flying mail, barnstorming, ballooning, or even personal, this new and exciting machine accumulated fatalities. Records show the first known US aircraft accident. On Sept 17th 1908, a modified Wright Brothers aircraft crashed during a demonstration at Fort Myer, VA, seriously injuring pilot Orville Wright and killing the observer, U.S. Army Lt. Thomas E. Selfridge. There are several reasons for aircraft accidents, such as pilot error, maintenance, weather, and colliding with unknown obstacles, to name a few. With extreme rarity, some of these situations still happen today.

Colliding Into Unknown Obstacles:

Unknown obstacles such as unfamiliar mountain elevations, high electrical powerlines and towers, tall factory chimneys, etc. claimed the lives of many aviation pioneers.

In 1934, a pilot named Elrey Borge Jeppesen founded a company while working for Varney Air Lines (United Airlines). His company, along

with his wife and flight attendant, Nadine Jeppesen, worked together to create special up- to- date aeronautical charts for pilots to navigate in flight, which were mainly geared toward safety. Their aviation mapping system caught on well to the point where they were selling chart books for $10. Today, *"Jepp Charts"* are used in most cockpits.

40

ARTIFICIAL INTELLIGENCE (AI) AND THE AIRCRAFT TECHNICIAN

According to Oxford Languages, artificial intelligence is the theory and development of computer systems able to perform tasks that normally require human intelligence, such as visual perception, speech recognition, decision-making, and translation between languages. Without getting into depth, there are 4 types of AI:

1. Reactive Machines

Machines that have no memory and are task-specific, meaning that an input always delivers the same output. Netflix's recommendation engine is powered by learning models that process the data collected from a customer's viewing history to determine specific movies and TV shows that they will enjoy. Humans are creatures of habit.

2. Limited Memory Machines

Unlike reactive machines, limited memory can look into the past and monitor specific objects or situations over time. Then, these observations are programmed into the AI memory so that its actions can be performed based on both past and present. Self-driving cars are a good example of limited memory AI. They observe other cars on the road for their speed, direction, and proximity. This information is programmed as the car's representation of the world, such as knowing signs, curves, and bumps, along with receiving data for lane changing, so as not to get hit or cut off by another driver.

3. Theory of Mind

Obviously, the first 2 types currently exist. Theory of mind and self-aware AI are theoretical types that could be built in the future. With many examples, theory of mind AI machines could understand intentions and predict behavior, as if to simulate human relationships.

4. Self-Aware

Lastly, an AI machine that is designed to have a sense of self and a conscious understanding of its existence. This AI will exist until we are able to uncover the way the human brain's intelligence works and how memory, learning, and decision-making work.

Based on the above information, we still have a long way to go to make progress in those last 2 types. In addition, none of the 4 types has a little effect on your career as an aircraft technician. In fact, AI can only make your job easier and more efficient.

There are 6 ways to use AI in aircraft maintenance:

1. Maintenance Schedules, Documentation

When operating a large fleet of aircraft, paperwork is an absolute must for communication and safety. Technicians' documents are sometimes lost or not entered as necessary. AI makes a great assistant in tracking maintenance schedules and documentation through the use of Algorithms.

Reminders can be put in place for easy reference regarding inspections and auditing maintenance records.

2. Autonomous Performance Monitoring

Preventive maintenance is the key task for most large maintenance operations. For example, time change alerts on certain components, such as aircraft batteries. AI can handle large data inputs easily and efficiently. In addition, AI performance monitoring can detect signs of structural fatigue, such as corrosion, cracks, and bending.

3. Mechanical Failure Prediction

What's the difference between preventive and predictive maintenance? Preventive maintenance is the scheduled maintenance of a component replacement and maintenance task. Predictive maintenance is performed on an as-needed basis. AI feeds data from smart sensors into an algorithm that analyzes aircraft systems and components.

4. AI-Powered Visual Inspections

Routine visual inspections are a necessary and valuable part of aircraft maintenance. Using computer vision algorithms, technicians can scan the plane for signs of potential maintenance problems more efficiently and increase productivity. A smart image processing program can be useful for parts such as fuel tanks, rotors, welds, electronics, and composite components. AI can be trained to recognize physical signs of repair needed.

5. Maintenance Data Analysis

Data analytics and pattern recognition are AI's greatest strengths. Once again, Algorithms can often recognize patterns and trends in data sets considerably more rapidly and intuitively than a human could. For instance, technicians may replace a key component in a fleet. As flight hours accumulate, the aircraft begin suffering more maintenance issues. By analyzing maintenance and performance data with AI, the technicians could discover that the replacement parts they have been installing are causing mechanical problems in the aircraft.

6. Aircraft Performance Optimization

Addressing repair needs is not the only positive quality that AI has. It can improve performance out of the fleet. For example, optimizing more efficient energy or fuel consumption is an area that AI might pinpoint in a system. Technicians can be proactive in fine-tuning performance and predictive maintenance, allowing them to stay ahead of future repairs. Performance optimization quite possibly may even assist in helping maintenance maximize the life span of the aircraft.

41

CASE IN POINT (ADDITIONAL)

In the early 80s, I worked for a national FBO in Louisville, KY.

One evening at home while watching TV, I got a call from my manager. He asked me if I could oversee a small aircraft that had crash-landed on the runway.

When I got there, I recognized a Piper Cherokee Arrow (single-engine) aircraft with retractable landing gear. The plane was sitting on the runway with no landing gear showing. The first thing I suspected was that the gear didn't come down due to mechanical failure. When looking in the cockpit, the landing gear control handle was still in the *"gear up"* position. Since the pilot was still there, I asked him what had happened. He simply said, *"I forgot to put the gear handle down before landing."* (Shit happens!)

In the late 90s, while working the night shift, I was assigned to a Boeing 757-200 maintenance check headset duty. My job was to communicate with the cockpit from the ground and clear all flight control movement. I cleared the flaps, which are fixed to the rear of the wings, and told the cockpit to move them. Meanwhile, I had to perform a test inside the belly of the plane. When I got done with the test, I noticed a ladder stuck under the flaps. I knew who did it, but I didn't get him involved. I took full responsibility, which resulted in $80,000 in damages and 3 days off without pay. The letter of discipline stayed in my personal file for 12 calendar months.

In the early 2000s, while working overtime at one of the gates at Los Angeles Int'l Airport, A Boeing 737 Next-Generation aircraft had taxied out full of passengers. The pilot radioed in and said he had no FMC (Flight Management Computer) on the 1st Officer's Side. When I got in the cockpit, the fault code showed a component on the right engine had *"internal failure."* I told the supervisor on shift that, as per the maintenance manual, the component had to be changed and loaded with the latest software. The plane was grounded, and all passengers and luggage were removed. Due to time constraints, the decision was made to change planes.

In the early 80s, while working in Louisville, KY, a BAC 1-11 was in for overnight contract maintenance. I noticed a beautiful young blonde was assigned to dump the poop tank at the front of the aircraft. I noticed she was having a little trouble securing the nozzle locking mechanism before the dump. I politely asked her if she needed any help, and she said, *"No, I know what I'm doing."* I slowly moved back with caution, and when she pulled that dump valve handle, the nozzle wasn't fully locked, and the *"blue poop juice"* got all over her. To top it off, I was thinking about asking her out for a date!

At the same FBO above, I was later laid off under questionable circumstances. However, it turned out to be a blessing in disguise. The chief pilot of a corporation stationed in my previous work hangar offered me a business opportunity. He offered me an all-expense paid trip to Grand Rapids, MI, to lead a heavy check crew on one of their 20 Series Learjets. With my tools and luggage, off we flew in the very aircraft to be worked on. My previous co-workers were like WTF. On that three-and-a-half-hour flight, I rode right seat (1st Officer). Once leveling off at 35,000 ft., Tom (the captain) said, *"Can you see the aircraft crossing us from the left?"* I said, *"No."* He said, *"Look really hard."* I saw this tiny speck hauling ass. It was a DC-10 about

50 miles away! Wow! The repair station maintenance crew and I worked about 2 weeks on the aircraft and flew it back to Louisville. In addition, the maintenance manager shared with me how to open my own maintenance facility; I guess he saw something in me at the time. Shortly after that, I got another job.

One of my most memorable experiences while working at Louisville Muhammad Ali International Airport (SDF), aka Standiford Field, was being there during Kentucky Derby Weekend. My assignment was to park the aircraft. All types of aircraft fly in for this event. At that time, there were so many planes that had to be parked; only one runway was open. The remaining runways, taxiways, and grass were used for parking. For example, Learjets were lined up together in formation, and Gulfstream Jets did the same. Since the piston aircraft were much lighter, they could be parked in the grass. Obviously, I witnessed many celebrities and VIPs. After the Derby was over, they all flew out quickly.

Around the early 2000s, I had a Boeing 757-200 come in for an overnight check. The pilot write-up was, *"left electric hydraulic pump cycles on and off with switch in the off position."* The pump was just doing its own thing! Technical support suggested changing the pump. I decided to hold off on that. I pulled the wiring diagrams for that particular aircraft and noticed that there were 2 electronic relays associated with the left pump. When I located them while the pump was cycling on and off, I noticed the 2 relays just clicking away. I removed one, and the pump stopped cycling. I put it back in, and the problem continued. I removed the second relay, and the cycling stopped. I made the decision to replace both relays, and that fixed the problem. We saved the company some money that night.

One Saturday morning, while employed by a small jet charter company in Columbus, Ohio, in the early 1980s, I noticed an elderly gentleman with a young boy near the hangars tinkering with a sports car. So, I walked over and began the chat with him, and he told me that the boy was his grandson. The sports car was a Chevrolet Corvette Indianapolis 500 Pace Car. His name was Paul W. Tibbetts, the great aviator of WW2 and the President of our company.

In the mid-1990s, my company had a large fleet of McDonnell Douglas DC-10-30 wide-body aircraft. It came in several times with an autopilot problem called "Pitch Porpoise." This would drive pilots nuts because it would usually happen during final approach, whereas unstable flight conditions already exist. Usually, a computer or an electro/hydraulic mechanical component would take care of the problem. Those components had already been replaced a couple of times. At this point, it's possibly a wiring problem. The wiring in this system is approximately 150' or so in length. Once I located the exact set of wires in that autopilot, resistance checks were performed. After all the wires were checked, I found one wire that read 8 ohms. From my experience, the reading was too high. We grounded the aircraft and replaced that one long wire. The long maintenance history on that system was cleared.

In 2015, a 737 Next Generation came in for an overnight check. Included with the check the crew wrote up, *"#1 engine thrust reverser will not deploy or stow."*

On this particular aircraft, the engine thrust reverser system comes with a fault indication box in the electronics compartment. Occasionally, this box will show a fault light in order to point you in a logical direction of the problem. However, in this case, it wasn't much help. Thrust reverser systems are divided electrically into two sub-systems: stow and deploy. While studying the wiring diagrams, I noticed there were electronic relays that controlled activation. Now here is the tough part. I had to find where the relay is actually located on the plane. Avionics engineers position electronic relays in multiple areas of the plane. Many of them are about one-fourth the size of a *"tic-tac"* box. After an hour or so, I finally located this tiny *"deploy"* relay behind a pressurized panel on the left side of the nose landing gear wheel well. I replaced the relay, and the T/R worked, and the write-up was cleared.

42

GENERAL AVIATION (GA)

According to two leading employment firms as of late 2025, there are approximately 5,700 (Glassdoor.com) and 3,700 (Indeed.com) job openings in the field of Aircraft Maintenance. A large percentage of these positions are in the area of General Aviation.

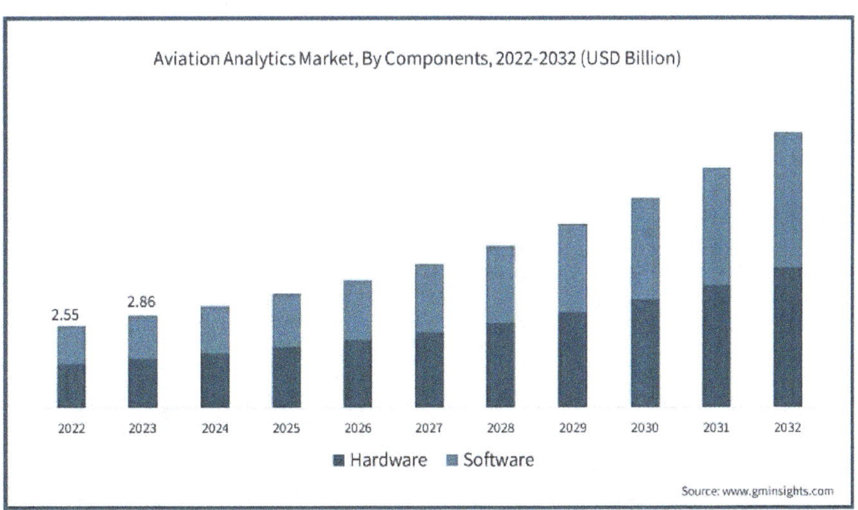

What is General Aviation (GA)?

To put it simply, General Aviation is categorized as a civilian, non-commercial flight. To break it down even further, GA consists of sport and recreational aviation, business travel, flying in support of humanitarian aid, environmental conservation or agriculture, bush flying, etc. However, GA is not military air operations, scheduled airline flights, or scheduled commercial air cargo flights. In relation to the aircraft maintenance field, all of these categories are under the strict rules and guidelines of the FAA/FAR requirements.

How did General Aviation get its start?

In the early 1900s, flying an aircraft was just a novelty, and only a few people owned airplanes. Prior to the 1930s, private flying was a rich man's sport or working pilots who flew more expensive planes (ex, Bill Boeing, Walter Varney, Charles Lindbergh). Around this time, General Aviation saw a rapid growth due to 3 aircraft manufacturers, aka known as The Big Three: Beechcraft, Cessna, and Piper. The first *"Model T"* of the aircraft industry was the Taylor E-2 Cub, which had only four instruments and a fuel gauge. The manufacturer was the Taylor Aircraft Co. out of Bradford, PA. The sale price for this aircraft was a whopping $1,425.00 and $1,495.00 with a choice of engines. In today's money, that's $29,000.00!

To give you an idea of the size and magnitude of the area, here are some facts and figures according to the National Air and Space Museum and the Texas A&M Transportation Institute:

- There are more than 340,000 GA aircraft around the world. U.S. pilots operate 204,000 of them.

- There are about 591,000 civilian pilots in the United States- and 70% of them fly GA planes.

- U.S. Forest Service firefighting consists of several flight divisions around the U.S.

- Pilots fly gliders, helicopters, corporate jets, and backcountry floatplanes.

- There are 221,000 GA aircraft in the U.S., approximately 92 percent of the total civilian aircraft fleet. Approximately 78 percent of all GA planes have fewer than 6 seats and weigh less than a compact automobile. *(2002)*

- GA generates around $65 billion a year in total national economic activity. *(2002)*

- GA connects the majority of communities with the national air transportation system. *(2002)*

- GA serves more than 5,300 public-use airports in communities large and small. Scheduled airlines go to about 660 U.S. airports. However, 75 percent of major airline flights operate out of just 46 big-city airports, and half of those flights move passengers between 29 hub airports. *(2002)*

I spent the first 5 years of my career in General Aviation: Columbus, Ohio, Louisville, KY, Indianapolis, IN, and Los Angeles, CA. These operators were subdivided in GA as Repair Stations and Jet Charter outfits. It was a great time learning my craft and working with very nice people.

Case in Point

As a young man working at an FBO in Columbus, Ohio, while going to Technical College in the early 1980s, I heard a loud screeching noise somewhere near the runway. On this day, it happened to be a quiet Saturday morning and raining. A few minutes later, a young man appeared out of nowhere, soaking wet, confused, with a puzzled look on his face. I asked, *"Are you ok?"* and he said, *"Yes, I'm fine, but I had an accident with my plane."* I asked him what happened, and he said, *"I caught a sudden tailwind and the propeller scraped the ground during touchdown."* We eventually towed the Cessna 172 to the hangar. Other than all the propeller blades completely curled and bent at the ends, the plane looked ok. Unfortunately, when there is a *"Prop Strike,"* the entire engine will have to be torn down to do a *"non-destructive inspection"* on its crankshaft to check for microscopic cracks. A very expensive bo-bo.

In the early 1980s, I got an opportunity of a lifetime and was able to hire on part-time with an FBO/Repair Station/Flight School in Columbus, Ohio. They were allowed to show up for work when I got out of my Technical College classes. Showing up to work one day, the Aircraft Maintenance Manager, who was a licensed pilot, asked me, *"Bob, have you ever flown in an aircraft before?"* At that time, I actually had not. So, he said, *"All of my mechanics have to have flown on the planes he repairs."* We immediately went on a test flight of a customer's Beechcraft *"V-tail"* Bonanza. While flying, my maintenance manager said the Bonanza is a *"Top of the Line"* in single-engine aircraft. Now that was a memorable experience!

Conclusion

One of the most satisfying parts of my career was mastering my craft. While doing so, I became able to sign my name and release an aircraft back into the air with confidence and safety as if one of my family members was on each and every one. Being able to leave my shift with the comfort that my co-workers, management staff, and quality control respect how I performed my work each day. And once I got home, I was able to sleep well with a clear conscience. I am very happy that I chose this satisfying career.

WHY I WROTE THIS BOOK

An Aviation Maintenance Technician or Mechanic is the *"behind the scenes"* part in many aviation stories and news. We hear so much about the pilots but very little about the technicians who keep the plane in the air! From a career standpoint, aviation maintenance can be very stable, with great pay and benefits, and self-gratifying. I feel that you will enjoy the in-depth perspective never expressed in this manner.

THE MECHANIC'S CREED

Upon my honor, I swear that I shall hold in sacred trust the rights and privileges conferred upon me as a certified mechanic. Knowing full well that the safety and lives of others are dependent upon my skill and judgment, I shall never knowingly subject others to risks which I would not be willing to assume for myself, or for those dear to me.

In discharging this trust, I pledge myself never to undertake work or approve work which I feel to be beyond the limits of my knowledge, nor shall I allow any non-certificated superior to persuade me to approve aircraft or equipment as airworthy against my better judgment, nor shall I permit my judgment to be influenced by money or other personal gain, nor shall I pass as airworthy aircraft or equipment about which I am in doubt, either as a result of direct inspection or uncertainty regarding the ability of others who have worked on it to accomplish their work satisfactorily.

I realize the grave responsibility which is mine as a certified airman, to exercise my judgment on the airworthiness of aircraft and equipment. I therefore pledge unyielding adherence to these precepts for the advancement of aviation and for the dignity of my vocation.

Flight Safety Foundation
Written by Jerome Lederer
Director, Safety Bureau
U.S. Civil Aeronautics Board, 1941

RESUME (SAMPLE)

OBJECTIVE

Lead, train, and perform maintenance duties on all high-performance aircraft.

EDUCATION

COLUMBUS TECHNICAL INSTITUTE, Columbus, Ohio

>Associate in Applied Science and FAA Airframe and Powerplant License (1981)

CATHEDRAL LATIN SCHOOL, Cleveland, Ohio

> Diploma

SCHOOLS/ TRAINING

Large Aircraft (A&P/ Avionics)

- *Boeing* 707-123/323; 727-100/200; 737-200/300/500/700/800/900; 747-100/200; 757-100/200/300
- *McDonnell Douglas* DC9-10/30; MD80; DC10-10/30; KC10
- *AIRBUS* A300
- *Lockheed* L-1011
- *B.A.C.* 1-11

Small Aircraft

- *Learjet* 20 and 30 Series
- *Beechcraft, Cessna, Piper*

EXPERIENCE

April 1985 to Present

CONTINENTAL AIRLINES, Los Angeles, California

> Airframe and Powerplant and Avionics Technician

> Acting Lead (Avionics)

February 1984 to February 1985

AMERICAN TRANS AIR, Indianapolis, Indiana

> Airframe and Powerplant Technician

February 1982 to February 1984

BUTLER AVIATION, Louisville, Kentucky

>Lead Airframe and Powerplant Technician

January 1979 to February 1982

EXECUTIVE JET AVIATION(NETJETS), Columbus, Ohio

> Airframe and Powerplant Technician

REFERENCES Available upon request

GLOSSERY

FBO	Fix Based Operator
MEL	Minimum Equipment List
FAA	Federal Aviation Administration
Servo	An electromechanical unit
POB	Portable Oxygen Bottle
CAA	Civil Aeronautics Authority
FAR	Federal Aviation Regulations
IPC	Illustrated Parts Catalog
IFE	In Flight Entertainment

REFERENCES

wikiland.com, "1877 Granite Cutters' 1st Health Plan"

temple.manifoldapp.org "The AFL and the Color Line"

publicintegrity.org "Low Paid Workers Are Unionizing"

"Homestead Strike of 1892" by Arthur Burgoyne

arnolditkin.com "4 Dangers Caused by Too Much Overtime"

teambuilding.com "Workplace Complacency Definition, Causes and Solutions"

aviationweek.com "Mechanic Safety Has Improved, But Significant Risks Remain"

washingtonpost.com "Labor Day: During FDR's New Deal, America debated between a 30-hour and 40-hour Workweek."

fluxpower.com "Aircraft Ground Handling in Cold Weather"

vimeo.com/420492939 "The Mechanician" A Brief History of Charles P. Taylor

skillkintl.com "How much is Your Aircraft Part Inventory Costing You?"

simpleflying.com "A Million Dollar Industry: How Much do Major Aircraft Engines Cost?"

en.m.wikipedia.org "Flight Simulator"

boeing.com "Boeing 787 Dreamliner"

sgpglobal.com "US Corporate Bankruptcy Filings Hit 12-year High in 1st 2 Months of 2023"

en.m.wikipedia.org "List of Airline Bankruptcies In The US"

onlinelibrary.wiley.com "History of Mergers"

investopedia.com "Mergers and Acquisitions(M&A): Types, Structures, Variations"

nigms.nih.gov "Circadian Rhythms-Nat'l Institute of General Medical Sciences"

bankrate.com "US Commuting Facts and Statistics"

cdc.gov "About Occupational Hearing Loss"

sensear.com "Top 7 Occupations Susceptible to Noise-Induced Hearing Loss" goodlogisticsgroup.com "History of Air Freight"

search.proquest.com "Fred Smith Thesis"

vxazegihe.wordpress.com "Fred Smith Thesis"

en.m.wikipedia.org "Howard Hughes"

latimes.com "G. Kruska; Spruce Goose Worker"

en.m.wikipedia.org "Hughes H-1 Racer"

thegreatharryhoudini.com "Harry Houdini-Aviation"

en.m.wikipedia.org "Bessie Coleman"

astronomy.com "Why Did NASA Retire the Space Shuttle?"

www.nasa.gov "The Space Shuttle"

uk.usembassy.gov "5 Experiments on the Int'l Space Station"

en.m.wikipedia.org "Scientific Research on the Int'l Space Station"

theatlantic.com "A Space Shuttle on the Streets of Los Angeles"

cars.com "Tundra Tugs Space Shuttle on the Streets of Los Angeles"

en.m.wikipedia.org "In-Flight Entertainment"

theguardian.com "Boeing Starts Costly Repair to Dreamliner Batteries"

afhistory.af.mil "1908-1st Fatality in a Powered Aircraft-Airforce Historical Support Division"

en.m.wikipedia.org "Jeppesen"

en.m.wikipedia.org "Paul Tibbets"

coursera.org "4 types of AI: Getting to Know Artificial Intelligence"

runwaysmag.com "Six Ways to use AI in Aircraft Maintenance"

airandspace.si.edu "What is General Aviation?"

The Age of Flight: A History of America's Pioneering Airline, by William Garvey and David Fisher

Texas A & M Transportation Institute (Aviation Research), "What is General Aviation?"